KORN SHELL

Quick Reference Guide

by Anatole Olczak

ASP, Inc.

PO Box 23837
San Jose California USA 95131
(800) 777-UNIX

ISBN 0-935739-21-1

NOTICE

Although the author and publisher have made every attempt to verify the accuracy of this book, the publisher and author cannot assume any liability for errors or ommissions. No warranty or other guarantee can be given as to the accuracy or suitability of this documentation for a particular purpose, nor can the author or publisher be liable for any loss or damage connected with, or arising out of, the furnishing, performance, or the use of the materials in this book. All information in this publication is subject to change without notice.

OTHER PUBLICATIONS AND SERVICES

ASP offers a full line of technical reference manuals, guides, and quick reference cards for UNIX, C/C++, Internet, and other topics. They are specifically designed for the professional who needs easy-to-access reference information to increase productivity. Please call or email (books@aspinc.com) for more information.

Korn Shell User and Programming Manual
UNIX Quick Reference Guide
Bourne Shell Quick Reference Guide
C Shell Quick Reference
JavaScript Quick Reference Guide
Tcl Quick Reference Guide
HTML, C, C++, SCCS, and Vi Quick Reference Cards

CONVENTIONS

Control characters are given as **Ctl** followed by the character in boldface. For example, **Ctl-d** specifies **Control-d** and is entered by pressing the **d** key while holding down the **Control** key. **Boldface** indicates items which must be typed exactly as given, *Italics* indicate items that are to be substituted, and [brackets] indicate optional items.

CONTENTS

INTRODUCTION

The Korn shell is an interactive command and programming language that provides an interface to UNIX and other systems. As an interactive command language, it is responsible for reading and executing the commands that you enter at your terminal. As a programming language, its special commands allow you to write sophisticated programs. It also provides the ability to customize your working environment.

The Korn shell offers compatibility with the Bourne shell, while providing a more robust programming language and command interpreter. It also contains some features of the C shell. Some of the major features of the Korn shell are:

- ▲ Improved performance
- ▲ Bourne shell compatibility
- ▲ Command-line editing
- ▲ Command history
- ▲ Enhanced I/O facilities
- ▲ Added data types and attributes
- ▲ Integer arithmetic support
- ▲ Arrays
- ▲ Improved string manipulation facilities
- ▲ Job control
- ▲ Aliases and functions
- ▲ Enhanced directory navigation facilities
- ▲ Enhanced debugging features

COMMAND EXECUTION

The primary prompt (**PS1** - default **$** or **#** for super-users) is displayed whenever the Korn shell is ready to read a command. The secondary prompt (**PS2** - default **>**) is displayed when the Korn shell needs more input.

Command Execution Format

command1 ; *command2*
> execute *command1* followed by *command2*

command &
> execute *command* asynchronously in the background; do not wait for completion

command1 | *command2*
> pass the standard output of *command1* to standard input of *command2*

command1 && *command2*
> execute *command2* if *command1* returns zero (successful) exit status

command1 || *command2*
> execute *command2* if *command1* returns non-zero (unsuccessful) exit status

command |&
> execute *command* asynchronously with its standard input and output attached to the parent shell; use **read –p/print –p** to manipulate the standard input/output

command \
> continue *command* onto the next line

{ *command* ; }
> execute *command* in the current shell

(*command*)
> execute *command* in a subshell

1

REDIRECTING INPUT/ OUTPUT

The Korn shell provides a number of operators that can be used to manipulate command input/output, files, and co-processes.

I/O REDIRECTION OPERATORS

<file	redirect standard input from *file*
>file	redirect standard output to *file*. Create *file* if non-existent, else overwrite.
>>file	append standard output to *file*; create if non-existent.
>|file	redirect standard output to *file*. Create *file* if non-existent, else overwrite even if **noclobber** is set.
<>file	open *file* for reading and writing as standard input
<&−	close standard input
>&−	close standard output
<&n	redirect standard input from file descriptor *n*
>&n	redirect standard output to file descriptor *n*
n<file	redirect file descriptor *n* from *file*
n>file	redirect file descriptor *n* to *file*
n>>file	redirect file descriptor *n* to *file*. Create *file* if non-existent, else overwrite.
n>|file	redirect file descriptor *n* to *file*. Create *file* if non-existent, else overwrite even if **noclobber** is set.
n<&m	redirect file descriptor *n* from file descriptor *m*
n>&m	redirect file descriptor *n* to file descriptor *m*
n<>file	open *file* for reading and writing as file descriptor *n*
n<<word	redirect to file descriptor *n* until *word* is read
n<<−word	redirect to file descriptor *n* until *word* is read; ignore leading tabs
n<&−	close file descriptor *n* for standard input
n>&−	close file descriptor *n* for standard output
*n<&**p**	redirect input from co-process to file descriptor *n*. If *n* is not specified, use standard input.
*n>&**p**	redirect output of co-process to file descriptor *n*. If *n* is not specified, use standard output.

FILENAME SUBSTITUTION

File name substitution is a feature which allows special characters and patterns to substituted with file names in the current directory, or arguments to the **case** and [[...]] commands.

PATTERN-MATCHING CHARACTERS/ PATTERNS

?	match any single character
*	match zero or more characters, including null
[abc]	match any characters between the brackets
[x–z]	match any character or characters in the range **x** to **z**
[a–c e–g]	match any characters in the range **a** to **c**, **e** to **g**
[!abc]	match any characters not between the brackets
[!x–z]	match any characters not in the range **x** to **z**
.	strings starting with **.** must be explicitly matched
?(*pattern-list*)	match zero or one occurrence of any *pattern*
*(*pattern-list*)	match zero or more occurrences of any *pattern*
+(*pattern-list*)	match one or more occurrence of any *pattern*
@(*pattern-list*)	match exactly one occurrence of any *pattern*
!(*pattern-list*)	match anything except any *pattern*
pattern-list	multiple patterns must be separated with a | character

VARIABLES

Like in other high-level progamming languages, variables are used by the Korn shell to store values. Variable names can begin with an alphabetic or underscore character, followed by one or more alphanumeric or underscore characters. Other variable names that contain only digits or special characters are reserved for special variables (called *parameters*) set directly by the Korn shell. Data types (called *attributes*) and one-dimensional arrays are also supported by the Korn shell.

VARIABLE/ATTRIBUTE ASSIGNMENT FORMAT

variable=   declare *variable* and set it to null

typeset *variable*=

declare *variable* and set it to null. If used within a function, then a local variable is declared.

variable=*value*   assign *value* to *variable*

typeset *variable*=*value*

assign *value* to *variable*. If used within a function, then a local variable is declared.

typeset −*attribute* *variable*=*value*

assign *attribute* and *value* to *variable*

typeset −*attribute* *variable*

assign *attribute* to *variable*

typeset +*attribute* *variable*

remove *attribute* from *variable* (except **readonly**)

VARIABLE/ATTRIBUTE LISTING FORMAT

typeset −*attribute*

display a list of variable names and their values that have attribute set

typeset +*attribute*

display a list of variable names that have attribute set

VARIABLE ATTRIBUTES

Variables can have one or more attributes that specify their internal representation, scope, or the way they are displayed.

VARIABLE ATTRIBUTE ASSIGNMENT FORMAT

typeset **–H** *variable*
> Set UNIX to host-name file mapping for non-UNIX systems

typeset **–i** *variable*
> Set *variable* to be integer type

typeset **–i***n* *variable*
> Set *variable* to be integer type with base *n*

typeset **–l** *variable*
> Set *variable* to lower case

typeset **–L** *variable*
> Left justify *variable*; the field width is specified by the first assignment

typeset **–L***n* *variable*
> Left justify *variable*; set field width to *n*

typeset **–LZ***n* *variable*
> Left justify *variable*; set field width to *n* and strip leading zeros

typeset **–r** *variable*
> Set *variable* to be readonly (same as **readonly**)

typeset **–R** *variable*
> Right justify *variable*; the field width is specified by the first assignment

typeset **–R***n* *variable*
> Right justify *variable*; set field width to *n*

typeset **–RZ***n* *variable*
> Right justify *variable*; set field width to *n* and fill with leading zeros

typeset **–t** *variable*
> Set the user-defined attribute for *variable*. This has no meaning to the Korn shell.

typeset **–u** *variable*
> Set *variable* to upper case

typeset **–x** *variable*
> Automatically export variable to the environment (same as **export**)

typeset **–Z** *variable*
> Same as **typeset –RZ**

5

VARIABLE SUBSTITUTION

Variable values can be accessed and manipulated using variable expansion. Basic expansion is done by preceding the variable name with the $ character. Other types of expansion can be used to return portions or the length of variables, use default or alternate values, assign default or alternate values, and more.

VARIABLE EXPANSION FORMAT

${*variable*}   value of *variable*

${#*variable*}   length of *variable*

${*variable:-word*}

>value of *variable* if set and not null, else print *word*. If **:** is omitted, *variable* is only checked if it is set.

${*variable:=word*}

>value of *variable* if set and not null, else variable is set to *word*, then expanded. If **:** is omitted, *variable* is only checked if it is set.

${*variable:?*}   value of *variable* if set and not null, else print **"variable: parameter null or not set"**. If **:** is omitted, *variable* is only checked if it is set.

${*variable:?word*}

>value of *variable* if set and not null, else print value of *word* and exit. If **:** is omitted, *variable* is only checked if it is set.

${*variable:+word*}

>value of *word* if *variable* is set and not null, else nothing is substituted. If **:** is omitted, *variable* is only checked if it is set.

${*variable#pattern*}

>value of *variable* without the smallest beginning portion that matches *pattern*

${*variable##pattern*}

>value of *variable* without the largest beginning portion that matches *pattern*

${*variable%pattern*}

>value of *variable* without the smallest ending portion that matches *pattern*

${*variable%%pattern*}

>value of *variable* without the largest ending portion that matches *pattern*

SPECIAL PARAMETERS

Some special parameters are automatically set by the Korn shell, and usually cannot be directly set or modified.

SPECIAL PARAMETERS

$ #	number of positional parameters
$ @	all positional parameters (**"$1"**, **"$2"**, ..., **"$n"**)
$ *	all positional parameters (**"$1 $2 ... $n"**)
$?	exit status of the last command
$$	process id of the current shell
$ –	current options in effect
$!	process id of the last background command or co-process

7

SPECIAL VARIABLES

There are a number of variables provided by the Korn shell that allow you to customize your working environment. Some are automatically set by the Korn shell, some have a default value if not set, while others have no value unless specifically set.

SPECIAL VARIABLES

CDPATH	search path for **cd** when not given a full pathname (no default)
COLUMNS	window width for in-line edit mode and **select** command lists (default **80**)
EDITOR	pathname of the editor for in-line editing (default **/bin/ed**)
ENV	pathname of the environment file (no default)
ERRNO	error number returned by most recently failed system call (system dependent)
FCEDIT	default editor for the **fc** command
FPATH	search path for auto-loaded functions
	pathname of the history file
HISTFILE	pathname of the history file (default **$HOME/.sh_history**)
HISTSIZE	number of commands to save in the command history file (default **128**)
HOME	home directory
IFS	internal field separator (default space, tab, newline)
LINES	specifies column length for **select** lists
MAIL	name of mail file
MAILCHECK	specifies how often to check for mail (default **600** seconds)
MAILPATH	search path for mail files (no default)
OLDPWD	previous working directory

8

OPTARG	value of the last **getopts** option argument
OPTIND	index of the last **getopts** option argument
PATH	search path for commands (default **/bin:/usr/bin:**)
PPID	process id of the parent shell
PS1	primary prompt string (default $, #)
PS2	secondary prompt string (default >)
PS3	**select** command prompt (default #?)
PS4	debug prompt string (default +)
RANDOM	contains a random number
REPLY	contains the input to the **read** command when no variables are given
SECONDS	contains number of seconds since Korn shell invocation
SHELL	pathname of shell
TERM	specifies your terminal type (no default)
TMOUT	Korn shell timeout variable (default **0**)
VISUAL	pathname of the editor for in-line editing

9

ARRAY VARIABLES

One-dimensional arrays are supported by the Korn shell. On most systems, arrays can have a maximum of 512 elements. Array subscripts start at 0 and go up to 511. Any variable can become an array by simply referring to it with a subscript.

ARRAY VARIABLE ASSIGNMENT FORMAT

variable[0]=*value variable*[1]=*value* ... *variable*[*n*]=*value*

set −A *variable value0 value1* ... *valuen*

typeset *variable*[0]=*value variable*[1]=*value* ... *variable*[*n*]=*value*
> assign values to array variable elements

set +A *variable value0 value1* ... *valuen*
> reassign values to array variable elements

typeset −*attributes variable*[0]=*value variable*[1]=*value* ...
> *variable*[*n*]=*value*
> assign *attributes* and values to array variable
> elements

typeset −*attributes variable*
> assign *attributes* to array variable

typeset +*attributes variable*
> remove *attributes* from array variable
> (except **readonly**)

ARRAY VARIABLE EVALUATION

${*array*}, $*array*
> array element zero

${*array*[*n*]}
> array element *n*

${*array*[*]}, ${*array*[@]}
> all elements of an array

${#*array*[*]}, ${#*array*[@]}
> number of array elements

${#*array*[*n*]}   length of array element *n*

MISC SUBSTITUTION

$(command)   replace with the standard output of *command*

$((arithmetic-expression)

    replace with the result of *arithmetic-expression*

$(<file)   replace with the contents of *file*

`command`   replace with the standard output of *command*
                  (provided for compatibility with the Bourne shell)

~   replace with **$HOME**

~user   replace with the home directory of *user*

~ –   replace with **$OLDPWD** (previous directory)

~ +   replace with **$PWD** (current directory)

QUOTING

Quotes are used when assigning values containing whitespace or special characters, to delimit variables, and to assign command output. They also improve readability by separating arguments from commands.

'...'   remove the special meaning of enclosed characters
                  except '

"..."   remove the special meaning of enclosed characters
                  except $, ', and \

\c   remove the special meaning of character *c*

`command`   replace with the standard output of *command*
                  (provided for compatibility with the Bourne shell)

IN-LINE EDITORS

In-line editing provides the ability to edit the current or previous commands before executing them. There are three in-line editing modes available: **emacs**, **gmacs**, and **vi**. The **emacs** and **gmacs** modes are basically the same, except for the way **Ctl-t** is handled. The in-line editing mode is specified by setting the **EDITOR** or **VISUAL** variables, or with the **set –o** command. The editing window width is specified by the **COLUMNS** variable. For lines longer than the window width, a mark is displayed to notify position. The marks >, <, and * specify that the line extends to the right, left, or both sides of the window.

VI INPUT MODE COMMANDS

#, <BACKSPACE>	delete the previous character
Ctl-d	terminate the Korn shell
Ctl-v	escape the next character
Ctl-w	delete the previous word
Ctl-x, @	kill the entire line
<RETURN>	execute the current line
\	escape the next *erase* or *kill* character

VI MOTION EDIT COMMANDS

[n]h, [n]<BACKSPACE>	move left one character
[n]l, [n]<SPACE>	move forward one character
[n]b	move backward one word
[n]B	move backward one word; ignore punctuation
[n]w	move forward one word
[n]W	move forward one word; ignore punctuation
[n]e	move to the end of the next word
[n]E	move to end of next word; ignore punctuation
[n]fc	move forward to character c
[n]Fc	move backward to character c
[n]tc	move forward to character before character c
[n]Tc	move backward to character before character c
[n];	repeat the last **f**, **F**, **t**, or **T** command
[n],	repeat the last **f**, **F**, **t**, or **T** command, but in the opposite direction
0	move cursor to start of line
^	move cursor to first non-blank character in line
$	move cursor to end of line

VI SEARCH/EDIT HISTORY COMMANDS

[*n*]**G**	get last command (or command *n*)
[*n*]**j**, [*n*]**+**	get next command from history file
[*n*]**k**, [*n*]**−**	get previous command from history file
n	repeat last / or ? search
N	repeat last / or ? search, except in opposite direction
/*string*	search backward in the history file for command that matches *string*
?*string*	search forward in the history file for command that matches *string*

VI TEXT MODIFICATION COMMANDS

a	add text after the current character
A	append text to end of the current line
[*n*]**c** *X*, **c**[*n*]*X*	change current character up to the cursor position defined by *X*
[*n*]**d** *X*, **d**[*n*]*X*	delete current character up to the cursor position defined by *X*
[*n*]**y** *X*, **y**[*n*]*X*	copy current character up to the cursor position defined by *X* into buffer
X	used to define ending cursor position for **c**, **d**, or **y** commands

	b	backwards to beginning of word
	e	cursor to end of current word
	w	cursor to beginning of next word
	W B E	same as **w b e**, except ignore punctuation
	0	before cursor to end of current line
	$	cursor to end of current line

C	change current character to end of line
D	delete current character through end of line
i	insert text left of the current character
I	insert text before beginning of line
[*n*]**p**	put previously yanked/deleted text after cursor
[*n*]**P**	put previously yanked/deleted text before cursor
[*n*]**r***c*	replace current character with *c*
R	replace text from cursor to <ESCAPE>
S	delete entire line and enter input mode
yy	copy the current line into the buffer
[*n*]**x**	delete the current character
[*n*]**X**	delete the previous character
[*n*]**.**	repeat the last text modification command
[*n*]**~**	toggle the case of the current character
[*n*]**_**	append last word of previous **ksh** command
****	replace the current word with the filename that matches *word**. For unique matches, append a / to directories and " " (space) for files.

13

VI OTHER EDIT COMMANDS

u	undo the last text modification command
U	undo all text modification commands on the current line
[*n*]**v**	return the output of the **fc –e** command
Ctl-l	redisplay current line
Ctl-j	execute the current line
Ctl-m	execute the current line
#	insert a # (comment) at beginning of the current line
=	list the files that match the current *word**
*****	replace current word with the files that match *word**
@_ *c*	insert value of alias *c*

EMACS/GMACS IN-LINE EDITOR COMMANDS

Ctl-b	move left one character
Ctl-f	move right one character
Esc-b	move left one word
Esc-f	move right one word
Ctl-a	move to beginning of line
Ctl-e	move to end of line
Ctl-h	delete preceding character
Ctl-x	delete the entire line
Ctl-k	delete from cursor to end of line
Ctl-d	delete current character
Esc-d	delete current word
Ctl-w	delete from cursor to mark
Ctl-y	undo last delete (w/**Esc-p**)
Ctl-p	get previous command from history file
Ctl-n	get next command from history file
Ctl-o	execute current command line and get the next command line
Ctl-r*string*	search backward in history file for command that contains *string*
Ctl-c	change current character to upper case
Esc-c	change current word to upper case
Esc-l	change current character to lower case

14

Esc-p	save to buffer from cursor to mark
Esc-<SPACE>, Ctl-@	
	mark current location
Ctl-l	redisplay current line
Ctl-]c	move cursor forward to character c
Ctl-xCtl-x	interchange the cursor and mark
erase	delete previous character
Esc-Ctl-h	delete previous word
Esc-h	delete previous word
Ctl-t	transpose current and next character (**emacs**)
Ctl-t	transpose two previous characters (**gmacs**)
Ctl-j	execute the current line
Ctl-m	execute the current line
Esc-<	get the oldest command line
Esc->	get the previous command line
Esc-n	define numeric parameter n for the next command (command can be **Ctl-c, Ctl-d, Ctl-k, Ctl-n, Ctl-p, Ctl-r, Esc-., Ctl-]**c, **Esc-_, Esc-b, Esc-c, Esc-d, Esc-f, Esc-h, Esc-l, Esc-Ctl-h**)
Esc-c	insert value of alias _c (c cannot be **b, c, d, f, h, l**, or **p**)
Esc-., Esc-_	insert last word of previous command
Esc-Esc	replace the current word with the filename that matches word*. For unique matches, append a / to directories and " " (space) for files
Esc-=	list the files that match the current word*list the files that match the current word*
Ctl-u	multiply parameter of next command by 4
\	escape the next character
Ctl-v	display the version of the shell
Esc-#	insert a # (comment) at beginning of the current line

JOB CONTROL

Job control is a process manipulation feature found in the Korn shell. It allows programs to be stopped and restarted, moved between the foreground and background, their processing status to be displayed, and more. To enable job control, the **monitor** option must be enabled. By default, this is enabled on systems that support the job control feature. When a program is run in the background, a job number and process id are returned.

JOB CONTROL COMMANDS

bg	put the current stopped job in the background
bg %n	put the stopped job n in the background
fg	move the current background job into the foreground
fg %n	move background job n into the foreground
jobs	display the status of all jobs
jobs –l	display status of all jobs along with their process ids
jobs –p	display the process ids of all jobs
kill –l	list all valid signal names
kill [–signal] %n	send the specified signal to job n (default 9)
set –m, set –o monitor	enable job control
stty [–]tostop	allow/prevent background jobs from generating output
wait	wait for all background jobs to complete
wait %n	wait for background job n to complete
Ctl-z	stop the current job

JOB NAME FORMAT

%n	job n
%+, %%	current job
%–	previous job
%string	job whose name begins with string
%?string	job that matches part or all of string

ARITHMETIC

Integer arithmetic is performed with the **let** and **((...))** commands. All of the operators from the C programming language (except ++, —, and ?:) are supported by the Korn shell. The format for arithmetic constants is:

number or *base#number*

where *base* is a decimal number between **2** and **36** that specifies the arithmetic base. If not specified, the default is base **10**. The arithmetic base can also be set with the **typeset –i** command.

ARITHMETIC COMMANDS

let "*arithmetic-expression*"
((*arithmetic-expression***))**   evaluate arithmetic expression
integer *variable*   declare an integer variable
integer *variable=integer-value*

    declare an integer variable and set it to a value

integer *variable="arithmetic-assignment-expression"*

    declare an integer variable and assign it the value of the
    arithmetic-assignment-expression

typeset –i*n variable[=value]*

    declare a base *n* integer variable, and optionally assign it a value

ARITHMETIC OPERATORS

–	unary minus
!	logical negation
~	bitwise negation
*, /, %	multiplication, division, remainder (modulo)
+, –	addition, subtraction
<<, >>	left shift, right shift
<=, <	less than or equal to, less than
>=, >	greater than or equal to, greater than
==, !=	equal to, not equal to
&	bitwise AND
^	bitwise exclusive OR
|	bitwise OR
&&	logical AND
||	logical OR
=	assignment
*=, /=, %=	multiply assign, divide assign, modulo assign
+=, –=	increment, decrement
<<=, >>=	left shift assign, right shift assign
&=, ^=, |=	bitwise AND assign, bitwise exclusive OR assign, bitwise OR assign
(...)	grouping (used to override precedence rules)

OPTIONS

The Korn shell has a number of options that specify your environment and control execution. They can be enabled/disabled with the **set** command or on the **ksh** command line.

ENABLING/DISABLING OPTIONS

ksh [–/+*options*]
> enable/disable the specified options

set [–/+*options*]
> enable/disable the specified options

LIST OF OPTIONS

–a	automatically export variables that are defined
–b	execute all background jobs at a lower priority
–c *cmds*	read and execute *cmds* (w/**ksh** only)
–e	execute **ERR** trap (if set) on non-zero exit status from any commands
–f	disable file name expansion
–h	make commands tracked aliases when first encountered
–i	execute in interactive mode (w/**ksh** only)
–k	put variable assignment arguments in environment
–m	enable job control (system dependent)
–n	read commands without executing them
–o allexport	automatically export variables that are defined
–o bgnice	execute all background jobs at a lower priority
–o emacs	use emacs-style editor for in-line editing
–o errexit	execute **ERR** trap (if set) on non-zero exit status from any commands
–o gmacs	use gmacs-style editor for in-line editing
–o ignoreeof	do not exit on end of file (default **Ctl-d**); use **exit**
–o keyword	put variable assignment arguments in the environment
–o markdirs	display trailing / on directory names resulting from file name substitution
–o monitor	enable job control (system dependent)
–o noclobber	prevent I/O redirection from truncating existing files

−o noexec	read commands without executing them
−o noglob	disable file name expansion
−o nolog	do not save function definitions in history file
−o nounset	return error on substitution of unset variables
−o privileged	disable processing of **$HOME/.profile**, and use **/etc/suid_profile** instead of **ENV** file
−o trackall	make commands tracked aliases when first encountered
−o verbose	display input lines as they are read
−o vi	use vi-style editor for in-line editing
−o viraw	process each character as it is typed in vi mode
−o xtrace	display commands and arguments as executed
−p	disable processing of **$HOME/.profile**, and use **/etc/suid_profile** instead of **ENV** file
−r	run a restricted shell (w/**ksh** only)
−s	read commands from standard input (w/**ksh** only)
−t	exit after reading and executing one command
−u	return error on substitution of unset variables
−v	display input lines as they are read
−x	display commands and arguments as executed
−	disable **−v** and **−x** flags; don't process remaining flags

ALIASES

Aliases are command macros and are used as shorthand for other commands, especially frequently-used ones.

ALIAS COMMANDS

alias   display a list of aliases and their values

alias *name*   display the value for alias *name*

alias *name*='*value*'
                        create an alias *name* set to *value*

alias –t   display a list of tracked aliases

alias –t *name*='*value*'
                        create a tracked alias *name* set to *value*

alias –x   display a list of exported aliases

alias –x *name*='*value*'
                        create an exported alias *name* set to *value*

unalias *name*   remove the alias name

SOME PRESET ALIASES

Alias	Value	Definition
autoload	typeset –fu	define an autoloading function
echo	print –	display arguments
functions	typeset –f	display list of functions
hash	alias –t –	display list of tracked aliases
history	fc –l	list commands from history file
integer	typeset –i	declare integer variable
r	fc –e –	re-execute previous command
stop	kill –STOP	suspend job
type	whence –v	display information about commands

CONDITIONAL EXPRESSIONS

The [[...]] command is used to evaluate conditional expressions with file attributes, strings, and integers. The basic format is:

[[*expression*]]

where *expression* is the condition you are evaluating. There must be whitespace after the opening brackets, and before the closing brackets. Whitespace must also separate the expression arguments and operators. If the expression evaluates to true, then a zero exit status is returned, otherwise the expression evaluates to false and a non-zero exit status is returned.

[[...]] STRING OPERATORS

-**n** *string*   true if length of *string* is not zero

-**o** *option*   true if *option* is set

-**z** *string*   true if length of *string* is zero

string1 = *string2*
                       true if *string1* is equal to *string2*

string1 != *string2*
                       true if *string1* is not equal to *string2*

string = *pattern*
                       true if *string* matches *pattern*

string != *pattern*
                       true if *string* does not match *pattern*

string1 < *string2*
                       true if *string1* is less than *string2*

string1 > *string2*
                       true if *string1* is greater than *string2*

[[...]] FILE OPERATORS

-a *file*	true if *file* exists
-b *file*	true if *file* exists and is a block special file
-c *file*	true if *file* exists and is a character special file
-d *file*	true if *file* exists and is a directory
-f *file*	true if *file* exists is a regular file
-g *file*	true if *file* exists and its setgid bit is set
-G *file*	true if *file* exists and its group id matches the current effective group id
-k *file*	true if *file* exists and its sticky bit is set
-L *file*	true if *file* exists and is a symbolic link
-O *file*	true if *file* exists and is owned by the effective user id
-p *file*	true if *file* exists and is a fifo special file or a pipe
-r *file*	true if *file* exists and is readable
-s *file*	true if *file* exists and its size is greater than zero
-S *file*	true if *file* exists and is a socket
-t *n*	true if file descriptor *n* is open and associated with a terminal device
-u *file*	true if *file* exists and its set user-id bit is set
-w *file*	true if *file* exists and is writable
-x *file*	true if *file* exists and is executable. If *file* is a directory, then true indicates that the directory is readable.
file1 -ef *file2*	true if *file1* and *file2* exist and refer to the same file
file1 -nt *file2*	true if *file1* exists and is newer than *file2*
file1 -ot *file2*	true if *file1* exists and is older than *file2*

[[...]] INTEGER OPERATORS

exp1 -eq *exp2*	true if *exp1* is equal to *exp2*
exp1 -ne *exp2*	true if *exp1* is not equal to *exp2*
exp1 -le *exp2*	true if *exp1* is less than or equal to *exp2*
exp1 -lt *exp2*	true if *exp1* is less than *exp2*
exp1 -ge *exp2*	true if *exp1* is greater than or equal to *exp2*
exp1 -gt *exp2*	true if *exp1* is greater than *exp2*

OTHER [[...]] OPERATORS

!*expression*	true if *expression* is false
(*expression*)	true if *expression* is true; used to group expressions
[[*expression1* && *expression2*]]	true if both *expression1* and *expression2* are true
[[*expression1* II *expression2*]]	true either *expression1* or *expression2* are true

CONTROL COMMANDS

case *value* **in**

> *pattern1*)   *commands1* ;;
> *pattern2*)   *commands2* ;;
>
> . . .
> *patternn*)   *commandsn* ;;

esac

Execute *commands* associated with the *pattern* that matches *value*.

for *variable* **in** *word1 word2 . . . wordn*
do

> *commands*

done

Execute *commands* once for each *word*, setting *variable* to successive *words* each time.

for *variable*
do

> *commands*

done

Execute *commands* once for each positional parameter, setting *variable* to successive positional parameters each time.

if *command1*
then

> *commands*

fi

Execute *commands* if *command1* returns a zero exit status.

if *command1*
then

> *commands2*

else

> *commands3*

fi

Execute *commands2* if *commands1* returns a zero exit status, otherwise execute *commands3*.

if *command1*
then
　　　　commands
elif *command2*
then
　　　　commands
. . .
elif *commandn*
then
　　　　commands
else
　　　　commands
fi

If command1 *returns a zero exit status, or* command2 *returns a zero exit status, or* commandn *returns a zero exit status, then execute the* commands *corresponding to the **if/elif** that returned a zero exit status. Otherwise, if all the **if/elif** commands return a non-zero exit status, execute the commands between **else** and **fi**.*

select *variable* **in** *word1 word2 . . . wordn*
do
　　　　commands
done

Display a menu of numbered choices word1 *through* wordn *followed by a prompt (**#?** or **$PS3**). Execute* commands *for each menu selection, setting* variable *to each selection and **REPLY** to the response until a **break**, **exit**, or EOF is encountered.*

select *variable*
do
　　　　commands
done

*Display a menu of numbered choices for each positional parameter followed by a prompt (**#?** or **$PS3**). Execute* commands *for each menu selection, setting* variable *to each selection and **REPLY** to the response until a **break**, **exit**, or EOF is encountered.*

until *command1*
do
　　　　commands
done

Execute commands *until* command1 *returns a zero exit status*

while *command1*
do
　　　　commands
done

Execute commands *while* command1 *returns a zero exit status.*

24

COMMANDS

:	null command; returns zero exit status
. *file*	read and execute the commands in *file* in the current environment
break	exit from the current enclosing **for, select, until,** or **while** loop
break *n*	exit from the *nth* enclosing **for, select, until,** or **while** loop
cd *dir*	change directory to *dir*. If *dir* not specified, change directory to **$HOME.**
cd *dir1 dir2*	change to directory where *dir1* in the current pathname is substituted with *dir2*
cd –	change directory to the previous directory
echo *args*	display arguments
eval *commands*	read and execute commands
exec *I/O-redirection-command*	
	perform I/O redirection on file descriptors
exec *command*	replace current process with *command*
exit	exit from the current program with the exit status of the last command. If given at the command prompt terminate the login shell.
exit *n*	exit from the current program with exit status *n*
export	display a list of exported variables
export *var=value*	
	set *var* to *value* and export
export *vars*	export *vars*
false	return a non-zero exit status
fc –l[*options*] [*range*]	

display *range* commands from the history file according to *options*. If no *range* argument is given, display the last 16 commands. Options can be:

    –n   do not display command numbers

    –r   reverse the order (latest commands first)

and *range* can be:

    n1 [*n2*] display list from command *n1* to command *n2*. If *n2* is not specified, display all commands from current command back to command *n1*.

    –*count* display the last *count* commands

    string display all the previous commands back to the command that matches *string*

fc [*options*] [*range*]

edit and re-execute range commands from the history file according to *options*. If no *range* argument is given, edit and re-execute the last command. Options can be:

–e *editor* use the specified editor (default **FCEDIT** or **/bin/ed**)

–r reverse the order (latest commands first)

and *range* can be:

n1 n2 edit command *n1* to command *n2*

n edit command *n*

–n edit previous *nth* command

string use all the previous commands back to the command that matches *string*

fc –e – [*old=new*] [*command*]

edit and re-execute *command* where *old=new* specified to replace the string *old* with *new* before executing. If no *command* argument is given, use the last command. The *command* can be given as:

n edit and re-execute command number *n*

–n edit and re-execute the last *nth* command

string edit and re-execute the most previous command that matches *string*

getopts *optsring name arguments*

parse *arguments*, using *optstring* as the list of valid options; save the option letter in *name*

getopts *optsring name*

parse positional parameters, using *optstring* as the list of valid options; save the option letter in *name*

newgrp change the group-id to the default group-id

newgrp *gid* change group id to *gid*

pwd display pathname of current directory

readonly display a list of readonly variables

readonly *var* set *var* to be readonly

readonly *var=value*

set *var* to *value* and make it readonly

set display a list of current variables and their values

set –o display current option settings

set *args* set positional parameters

set *–args* set positional parameters even if they begin with –

set –s sort positional parameters

set – – unset positional parameters

shift shift the positional parameters once to the left

shift *n* shift the positional parameters *n* times to the left
test *expression* evaluate *expression*
time *command* display the elapsed, user, and system time spent executing *command*
times display the total user and system time for the current Korn shell and its child processes
trap *commands signals*
  execute *commands* when *signals* are received
trap "" *signals* ignore *signals*
trap *signals*, **trap** *−signals*
  reset traps to their default values
trap *commands* **0**, **trap** *commands* **EXIT**
  execute *commands* on exit
trap display a list of current traps
trap *commands* **DEBUG**
  execute *commands* after each command is executed
trap *commands* **ERR**
  if the **errexit** (**−e**) option is enabled, then execute *commands* after commands that have a non-zero exit status
true return a non-zero exit status
typeset display a list of current variables and their values
ulimit [*options*] *n*
  set a resource limit to *n*. If *n* is not given, the specified resource limit is displayed. If no *option* is given, the file size limit (**−f**) is displayed.
  −a displays all the current resource limits
  −c *n* set the core dump size limit to *n* 512-byte blocks
  −d *n* set the data area size limit to *n* kilobytes
  −f *n* set the child process file write limit to *n* 512-byte blocks (default)
  −m *n* set the physical memory size limit to *n* kilobytes
  −s *n* set the stack area size limit to *n* kilobytes
  −t *n* set the process time limit to *n* seconds
umask display the current value of the file creation mask
umask *mask* set the default file creation mask to *mask*
unset *var* remove the definition of *var*
whence *name* display information about *name*
whence *−v* *name*
  display more information about *name*

FUNCTIONS

Functions are a form of commands like aliases, and scripts. They differ from Korn shell scripts, in that they do not have to read in from the disk each time they are referenced, so they execute faster. They also provide a way to organize scripts into routines, like in other high-level programming languages. Since functions can have local variables, recursion is possible. Functions are defined with the following format:

function *name* { *commands* ; }

Local function variables are declared with the **typeset** command within the function.

FUNCTION COMMANDS

return	return from a function
return *n*	return from a function; pass back return value of *n*
typeset –f	display a list of functions and their definitions
typeset +f	display a list of function names only
typeset –fu	display a list of autoloading functions
typeset –fu *name*	make function name autoloading
typeset –fx	display a list of exported functions
typeset –fx *name*	export function *name*
typeset –ft *name*	display function commands and arguments as they are executed
unset –f *name*	remove function *name*

THE PRINT COMMAND

print [*options*] *arguments*
> display *arguments* according to *options*

print Options

–	treat everything following – as an argument, even if it begins with –
–n	do not add a ending newline to the output
–p	redirect the given arguments to a co-process
–r	ignore the \ escape conventions
–R	ignore the \ escape conventions; do not interpret – arguments as options (except **–n**)
–s	redirect the given arguments to the history file
–u*n*	redirect arguments to file descriptor *n*. If the file descriptor is greater than **2**, it must first be opened with the **exec** command. If *n* is not specified, the default file descriptor is **1** (standard output).

print Escape Characters

\a	Bell character
\b	Backspace
\c	Line without ending newline
\f	Formfeed
\n	Newline
\r	Return
\t	Tab
\v	Vertical tab
\\	Backslash
\0*x*	8-bit character whose ASCII code is the 1-, 2-, or 3-digit octal number x

THE READ COMMAND

read [*options*] *variables*
> read input into *variables* according to *options*

read *name?prompt*
> display *prompt* and read the response into *name*

read Options

-p	read input line from a co-process
-r	do not treat \ as the line continuation character
-s	save a copy of input line in the command history file
-un	read input line from file descriptor *n*. If the file descriptor is greater than **2**, it must first be opened with the **exec** command. If *n* is not specified, the default file descriptor is 0.

MISC

#	anything following a # to the end of the current line is treated as a comment and ignored
#!*interpreter*	if the first line of a script starts with this, then the script is run by the specified interpreter
rsh	running under the restricted shell is equivalent to **ksh**, except that the following is not allowed: • changing directories • setting the value of **ENV**, **PATH**, or **SHELL** variables • specifying path or command names containing / • redirecting output of a command with >, >l, <>, or >>

DEBUGGING KORN SHELL SCRIPTS

The Korn shell provides a number of options that are useful in debugging scripts: **noexec** (**–n**), **verbose** (**–v**), and **xtrace** (**–x**). The **noexec** (**–n**) option causes commands to be read without being executed and is used to check for syntax errors. The **verbose** (**–v**) option causes the input to displayed as it is read. The **xtrace** (**–x**) option causes commands in Korn shell scripts to be displayed as they are executed. This is the most useful, general debugging option. For example, **tscript** could be run in trace mode if invoked "**ksh –x tscript**".

FILES

$HOME/.profile

> contains local environment settings, such as the search path, execution options, local variables, aliases, and more. At login time, it is read in and executed after the **/etc/profile** file.

$HOME/.sh_history

> contains previously executed commands

$ENV contains the name of the file that has aliases, function, options, variables, and other environment settings that are to be available to subshells

/etc/profile

> contains the system-wide environment settings, such as a basic search path, a default **TERM** variable, the system **umask** value, and more (system dependent). If existent, it is read in and executed at login time before the **$HOME/.profile** file.

/etc/suid_profile

> contains local and system environment settings for privileged mode (system dependent)

EXAMPLE COMMANDS

Execute multiple commands on one line
```
$ pwd ; ls tmp ; print "Hello world"
```
Run the **find** command in the background
```
$ find . -name tmp.out -print &
```
Connect the output of **who** to **grep**
```
$ who | grep fred
```
Talk to **fred** if he is logged on
```
$ { who | grep fred ; } && talk fred
```
Send **ls** output to **ls.out**, even if **noclobber** is set
```
$ ls >| ls.out
```
Append output of **ls** to **ls.out**
```
$ ls >> ls.out
```
Send **invite.txt** to **dick**, **jane**, and **spot**
```
$ mail dick jane spot < invite.txt
```
List file names that begin with **z**
```
$ ls z*
```
List two, three, and four character file names
```
$ ls ?? ??? ????
```
List file names that begin with **a**, **b**, or **c**
```
$ ls [a-c]*
```
List file names that do not end with **.c**
```
$ ls *[!.c]
```
List file names that contain any number of consecutive **x**'s
```
$ ls *(x)
```
List file names that contain only numbers
```
$ ls +([0-9])
```
List file names tha do not end in **.c**, **.Z**, or **.o**
```
$ ls !(*.c|*.Z|*.o)
```
Set **NU** to the number of users that are logged on
```
$ NU=$(who | wc -l)
```
Set **HOSTS** to the contents of the **/etc/hosts** file
```
$ HOSTS=$(</etc/hosts)
```
Set **TOTAL** to the sum of **4 + 3**
```
$ TOTAL=$((4+3))
```
Change directory to **jane**'s home directory
```
$ cd ~jane
```

Set the right-justify attribute on variable **SUM** and set it to **70**
```
$ typeset -R SUM=70
```
Set and export the variable **LBIN**
```
$ typeset -x LBIN=/usr/lbin
```
Set the field width of **SUM** to **5**
```
$ typeset -R5 SUM
```
Remove the lowercase attribute from **MSYS**
```
$ typeset +l MSYS
```
Unset variable **LBIN**
```
$ unset LBIN
```
Display the length of variable **FNAME**
```
$ print ${#FNAME}
```
Set **SYS** to the hostname if not set, then display its value
```
$ print ${SYS:=$(hostname)}
```
Display an error message if **XBIN** is not set
```
$ : ${XBIN:?}
```
Display the base directory in **LBIN**
```
$ print ${LBIN##*/}
```
Set array variable **MONTHS** to the month names
```
$ set -A MONTHS jan feb mar apr may . . . dec
```
Display element 3 of the **XBUF** array variable
```
$ print ${XBUF[3]}
```
Display the length of the **TMP** array element 2
```
$ print ${#TMP[2]}
```
Display **$HOME set to /home/anatole**
```
$ print '$HOME set to' $HOME
```
Display the value of **$ENV**
```
$ print $ENV
```
Display the last five commands from the history file
```
$ history -5
```
Retrieve last **print** command in vi edit mode
```
$ set -o vi; <ESCAPE>/^print<RETURN>
```
Bring background job 3 into the foreground
```
$ fg %3
```
Display all information about current jobs
```
$ jobs -l
```

33

\# Terminate job 5
```
$ kill %5
```

\# Increment variable **X**
```
$ integer X; ((X+=1))
```

\# Set variable **X** to **5** in base **2**
```
$ typeset -i2 X=5
```

\# Set variable **X** to **20** modulo **5**
```
$ ((X=20%5))
```

\# Set **Y** to **5*4** if **X** equals **3**
```
$ ((X==3 && (Y=5*4)))
```

\# Terminate the Korn shell if no input given in 30 minutes
```
$ TMOUT=1800
```

\# Automatically export variables when defined
```
$ set -o allexport
```

\# Set diagnostic mode
```
$ set -x
```

\# Create an alias for the **ls** command
```
$ alias l='ls -FAc | ${PAGER:-/bin/pg}'
```

\# Create a tracked alias for the **cp** command
```
$ alias -t cp
```

\# Put the command number and current directory in the prompt
```
$ typeset -x PS1="!:$PWD> "
```

\# Check if variable **X** is set to a number
```
$ [[ $X = +([0-9]) ]] && print "$X is a number"
```

\# Check if **VAR** is set to null
```
$ [[ -z $VAR ]] && print "VAR is set to null"
```

\# Check if **FILE1** is newer than **FILE2**
```
$ [[ $FILE1 -nt $FILE2 ]]
```

\# Check if **VAR** is set to **ABC**
```
$ [[ $VAR = ABC ]]
```

\# Check if the **bgnice** option is set
```
$ [[ -o bgnice ]] && print "bgnice option set"
```

\# Check if **TMP** is a readable directory
```
$ [[ -d $TMP && -x $TMP ]]
```

\# Check the number of arguments
```
$ (($# == 0)) && { print "Need arg"; exit 1; }
```

\# Display an error message, then beep
```
$ print "Unexpected error!\a"
```
\# Display a message on standard error
```
$ print -u2 "This is going to standard error"
```
\# Write a message to the command history file
```
$ print -s "su attempted on $(date)"
```
\# Take standard input from **FILE**
```
$ exec 0<FILE
```
\# Open file descriptor **5** for reading and writing
```
$ exec <>5
```
\# Display a prompt and read the reply into **ANSWER**
```
$ read ANSWER?"Enter response: "
```
\# Create a function **md** that creates a directory and **cd**'s to it
```
$ function md { mkdir $1 && cd $1 ; pwd }
```
\# Set a trap to ignore signals **2** and **3**
```
$ trap "" 2 3
```
\# Run **dbtest** in **noexec** mode
```
$ ksh -n dbtest
```
\# Set a trap to execute **pwd** after each command
```
$ trap "pwd" DEBUG
```
\# Set **X** to **1** and make it readonly
```
$ readonly X=1
```
\# Set **VAR** to **1** and export it
```
$ export VAR=1
```
\# Set the positional parametersto **A B C**
```
$ set A B C
```
\# Set the file size creation limit to 1000 blocks
```
$ ulimit 1000
```
\# Disable core dumps
```
$ ulimit -c 0
```
\# Add group write permission to the file creation mask
```
$ umask 013
```
\# Return information about the **true** command
```
$ whence -v true
```

EXAMPLE
KORN SHELL SCRIPTS

The **knl** script is the Korn shell version of the UNIX **nl** command. It displays line-numbered output.

```ksh
#!/bin/ksh
#
#    knl - Korn Shell line-numbering filter
#    A Olczak - ASP, Inc
#

# Initialize line number counter
integer LNUM=1

# Check usage
(($# == 0)) && { print "Usage: $0 file" ;exit 1 ; }

# Process each file
for FILE
do
     # Make sure file exists
     [[ ! -f $FILE ]] && { print no $FILE; exit 1; }

     # Open file for reading
     exec 0<$FILE

     # Read each line, display with line number
     while read -r LINE
     do
          print "$LNUM: $LINE"
          ((LNUM+=1))
     done

     # Reset line number counter
     LNUM=1
done
```

The **kcal** script implements a menu-driven calendar program. It supports addition, deletion, modification, and listing of calendar entries. It also provides the ability to find the calendar entry for the current day and list all calendar entries.

```ksh
#!/bin/ksh
#
#     kcal - Korn Shell calendar program
#
#     Anatole Olczak - ASP, Inc
#

# Process errors
function error {
    print ${1:-"unexplained error encountered"}
    exit ${2}
}

# Check arguments
if (($# > 0))
then
    error "Usage: $0" 1
fi

# Use environment variable setting or default
: ${CALFILE:=$HOME/.calfile}

# Create calendar file if non-existent; flag
# creation error
if [[ ! -f $CALFILE ]]
then
    print "Creating default $HOME/.calfile"
    > $HOME/.calfile || error "$HOME/.calfile: \
    cannot create" 1
fi

# Variable declaration/assignment
typeset DATE= LINE= ENTRY= REPLY="yes" \
PAGER=$(whence more) CLEAR=$(whence clear)

# Set trap to not allow interrupts
trap '$CLEAR; print "\aInterrupt ignored - use \
menu to quit.  Press <Return> to continue."; \
read TMP; $CLEAR' INT QUIT

# Set EXIT trap - perform cleanup
trap 'rm -rf /tmp/.FOUND$$ /tmp/.CHANGE$$ \
/tmp/.DEL$$' EXIT
```

37

```
# Check the date
function checkdate {
    while ((1))
    do
        # Prompt for date
        read DATE?"Enter date in mmdd[yy] format
(default today):"
        case $DATE in

            # Default - use todays date
            "" ) DATE=$(date +%m-%d-%y)
                break ;;

            # Check the given date
            +([0-9]) )
                case ${#DATE} in
                    4|6)
                        # Set month to 1st 2 chars
                        typeset -L2 MO=$DATE

                        # Check length for year;
                        # 4 = mmdd, 6 = mmddyy
                        if ((${#DATE} == 6))
                        then
                            # Set TMP to get date
                            typeset -L4 TMP=$DATE

                            # Get day
                            typeset -R2 DA=$TMP

                            # Get year
                            typeset -R2 YR=$DATE
                        else
                            # Get day
                            typeset -R2 DA=$DATE

                            # Set to current year
                            YR=$(date +%y)
                            DATE=$DATE$YR
                        fi

                        # Now check values.  DA
                        # must be in range 01-31
                        if ((DA < 01 || DA > 31))
                        then
                            print "$DA: invalid \
                            day format - try \
                            again"
                            continue
                        fi
```

```
                    # Month must be 01-12
                    if ((MO < 01 || MO > 12))
                    then
                        print "$MO: invalid \
                        month format - try  \
                        again"
                        continue
                    fi

                    # Set format mm-dd-yy
                    DATE=$MO-$DA-$YR
                    break ;;

            * ) # Invalid format
                    print "$DATE: invalid  \
                    format - try again" ;;

            esac ;;

    # Invalid date given
    * ) print "$DATE: invalid format - try again" ;;

    esac
    done
}

# Add new calendar entry
function addentry {
    $CLEAR
    ENTRY="$DATE"

    # For existent entry, just add more data
    COUNT=$(grep -c "^$DATE" $CALFILE)
    if ((COUNT > 0))
    then
        changeentry
        return
    fi

    # Prompt for input
    print "Enter info for $DATE: (enter <Return> by itself
when finished)"
    while ((1))
    do
        read LINE?"=>"
        if [[ -n $LINE ]]
        then
            ENTRY="$ENTRY,$LINE"
        else
            break
        fi
    done
```

```
        # Append to calendar file
        print  $ENTRY>>$CALFILE

        # Sort the calendar file
        sort  -o  $CALFILE  $CALFILE
}

function  formatentry  {
    $CLEAR

    typeset  IFS=","  \
      BORDER="*********************************"  \
    BORDER1="*                               *"  \
    FILE=$1

    if  [[  -s  $FILE  ]]
    then

        # Open calendar file for reading, and
        # format output
        (exec  0<$FILE
        while  read  -r  ENTRY
        do
            print  "$BORDER\n$BORDER1"
            set  $ENTRY
            typeset  -L35  LINE="DATE:  $1"
            print  "*  $LINE*"
            shift
            print  "$BORDER1"
            for  i
            do
                LINE="$i"
                print  "*  $LINE*"
            done
            print  "$BORDER1"
        done
        print  "$BORDER"
        )  |  $PAGER
    else
        print "No  entries  found."
    fi

    # Prompt to continue
    until  [[  $REPLY  =  ""  ]]
    do
        read  REPLY?"Enter  <Return>  to  continue..."
    done
}
```

```
# Find specific entry
function findentry {
    $CLEAR

    # Check for entry - put it in temp found file
    grep $DATE $CALFILE >/tmp/.FOUND$$

    # Format found entries
    formatentry /tmp/.FOUND$$
}

# Change an entry
function changeentry {

    # Find specific entry - put it in temp found file
    grep $DATE $CALFILE | tr ',' '\012'>/tmp/.FOUND$$

    # Return if no entry was found
    if [[ ! -s /tmp/.FOUND$$ ]]
    then
        $CLEAR
        read TMP?"Entry for $DATE not found - press
<Return> to continue"
        return
    fi

    # Prompt again for change
    while [[ $REPLY != "" ]]
    do
        read REPLY?Change/Add to entry for <$DATE>?
        case $REPLY in

            [yY]* | "" )
                break ;;

            [nN]* ) print Ok, aborting entry change
                return ;;

            * ) print Invalid reply - try again. ;;

        esac
    done

    # Edit the temporary found file
    ${EDITOR:-vi} /tmp/.FOUND$$

    # Remove the specified original entry
    grep -v $DATE $CALFILE > /tmp/.CHANGE$$
```

```
        # Put back new change in record format.
        # Add trailing \n
        (cat /tmp/.FOUND$$ | tr '\012' ',' ; print   ) \
        >>/tmp/.CHANGE$$

        # Put back new file
        cat /tmp/.CHANGE$$ > $CALFILE

        # Clean up tmp files
        rm -rf /tmp/.CHANGE$$ /tmp/.FOUND$$
}

# Remove specific entry
function delentry {

        # Look for entry
        grep $DATE $CALFILE >/tmp/.FOUND$$

        # Return if not found
        if [[ ! -s /tmp/.FOUND$$ ]]
        then
             $CLEAR
             read TMP?"Entry for $DATE not found - press
<Return> to continue"
             return
        fi

        # Prompt to delete
        while [[ $REPLY != "" ]]
        do
             read REPLY?"Delete entry for <$DATE>?"
             case $REPLY in
                 [yY]* | "" ) break ;;
                    [nN]* )print "ok, aborting delete";
return ;;
                    * ) print "Invalid reply - try again." ;;
             esac
        done

        # Merge changes - put them in temporary file
        grep -v $DATE $CALFILE > /tmp/.DEL$$

        # Put back new file
        cat /tmp/.DEL$$ > $CALFILE

        # Clean up tmp files
        rm -rf /tmp/.DEL$$ /tmp/.FOUND$$
}
```

```
# Set menu selection prompt
PS3="Enter selection or <Return> for default menu:"

# Display menu
while ((1))
do
      $CLEAR
      select i in "Add calendar entry" "Delete calendar
entry" "Change calendar entry" "Find calendar entry" "List
all calendar entries" "List todays calendar entry" "Exit"
      do
            case $i in

                  "Add calendar entry")
                     checkdate
                     addentry
                     $CLEAR ;;
                  "Delete calendar entry")
                     checkdate
                     delentry
                     $CLEAR ;;
                  "Change calendar entry")
                     checkdate
                     changeentry
                     $CLEAR ;;
                  "Find calendar entry")
                     checkdate
                     findentry
                     $CLEAR ;;
                  "List all calendar entries")
                     formatentry $CALFILE
                     $CLEAR ;;
                  "List todays calendar entry")
                     DATE=$(date +%m-%d-%y)
                     findentry
                     $CLEAR ;;
                  "Exit")
                     exit ;;
                  * ) print "\aInvalid selection \c"
                     read TMP?"- press <Return> to continue"
                     $CLEAR
                     continue ;;
            esac
      done
done
```

DOWNLOADABLE SCRIPTS AND TIPS

Selected examples of code from ASP publications are available for free downloading from the ASP website. Now you can study and customize these programs without tedious keyboarding.

To take advantage of this special ASP customer service, visit <www.aspinc.com> and click on the "Downloads" icon. After entering basic registration information, you will be taken to the Download Requests page where you may choose examples from a variety of ASP publications.

QUICK REFERENCE PUBLICATIONS FROM ASP

UNIX Quick Reference Guide

You don't need to fumble through oversized volumes for quick reference lookups. Get a concise reference guide to UNIX in a single, compact handbook. The *UNIX Quick Reference Guide* contains the user and many admin commands for UNIX, including Solaris and BSD, plus hundreds of examples.

Bourne Shell Quick Reference Guide

The Bourne Shell was the original shell for UNIX, and it still remains the most widely used and distributed. The *Bourne Shell Quick Reference Guide* summarizes this scripting language and includes complete sample programs and examples. Many UNIX commands used in Bourne Shell scripting are also included.

C Shell Quick Reference Guide

The C Shell was developed as a replacement for the standard Bourne shell and is found on most systems running UNIX. The *C Shell Quick Reference Guide* covers this scripting language and includes complete sample programs and examples. Many UNIX commands used in C Shell scripting are also included.

JavaScript Quick Reference Guide

JavaScript is a cross-platform, object-based scripting language for client and server applications. The *JavaScript Quick Reference Guide* covers this scripting language and includes complete sample programs and practical examples.

Tcl Quick Reference Guide

The *Tcl Quick Reference Guide* covers the Tool control language and includes complete sample programs and practical examples.

Quick Reference Cards

Vi, C, C++, SCCS, HTML Reference Cards

Multi-fold cards provide concise summaries for programmers and users.

For order information, email books@aspinc.com.